Angel Companions

CKE Publications
Olympia, Washington

About the Author...

I have always enjoyed crafts and enjoyed working with my hands. Over the years I have done sewing, needle-crafts, costuming, floral arranging, creating seashell projects and such. With a "can do" attitude, I have been successful in my stained glass design work. Vivid colors, nature itself, and the way light brings out the beauty of glass have been my inspiration. I believe that a sense of spirituality is expressed in these patterns.

I live in Pt. Ludlow, Washington with my husband and our cat, Zack, and enjoy traveling, reading science fiction and attending Bluegrass festivals. I plan to teach stained glass and continue my design work in this beautiful place.

This book is dedicated to the memory of my mother, Roberta Grace Bestrop, who encouraged my artistic abilities by her example, and my high school teacher and mentor, Kay Keyes, who gave me her friendship and encouragement throughout the years I knew her.

My gratitude extends to Deverie Wood (of Light in Glass Publishing), my stained glass teacher, advisor, and publishing guide. Many thanks go to Judy Johnson of Pt. Ludlow whose studio space enabled me to complete many of these angels on time.

My thanks also for the prayers and support of Pastor Lindsy Ireland of Community United Methodist Church of Pt. Hadlock and my church family of Northshore United Church of Christ of Woodinville, WA.

My final thanks go to our family and friends who helped support us through our home construction and Stephen's recovery from ankle surgery.
Most of all, I wish to thank Stephen, my best friend, whose constant love and support have been the best thing in my life.

Also, a huge thank-you to CKE Publications for their trust and belief in me as an artist and designer. Ladies, you've been great!

Questions or comments?
Contact the designer at Ponygal Productions, PO Box 65156, Pt. Ludlow, WA 98365 - (360) 437-7627

Every effort has been made to ensure that all information in this book is accurate. However, due to differing conditions, tools, and individual skills, the publisher and author cannot be responsible for any injuries, losses, or other damages that may result from the use of the information in this book.

Book Production: Laura Tayne
Printed in the U.S.A. by: Consolidated Press, Seattle, WA

ISBN 978-1-932327-25-0

Copyright © Pat Chase, 2007. Covers all patterns and text used in this publication.

All Rights Reserved. No part of this publication may be reproduced, stored or transmitted in any form or by any means, electronic, mechanical, recording or otherwise, without the prior permission of the copyright owner, with the exception of reproduction of the patterns for personal use only.
Notice to Copy Centers: Permission is given to enlarge any design in this book to the maximum of four copies per customer.

Distribution
CKE PUBLICATIONS
PO Box 12869
Olympia, WA 98508-2869
USA
Tel: (360) 352-4427 FAX: 360-943-3978
E-mail: ckepublications@comcast.net
Web: www.ckepublications.com

Call CKE at 1-800-428-7402 to ask for a free catalog of our books and patterns, also for information about our pattern enlargement service.

Basic Instructions . . .

You will find that the angels are easily built using basic stained glass construction and the additional information given below. Any special instructions will be included with individual patterns.

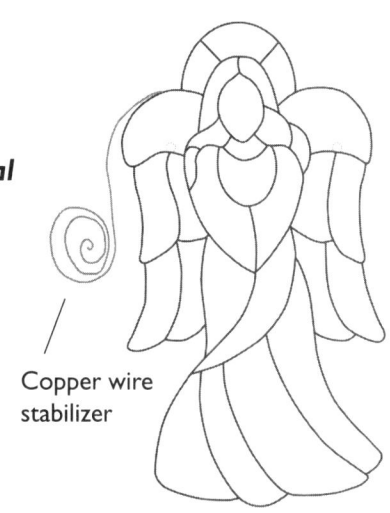
Copper wire stabilizer

- Cut, grind, foil and solder all glass pattern pieces. 3/16" copper foil is used on the insides of adjoining pieces. 7/32" copper foil is used on the outside edges to give a stronger edge. After your angel is completely soldered, add copper wire around the perimeter to give extra stability and strength.

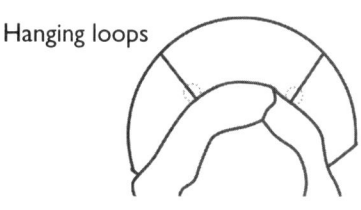
Hanging loops

- Hanging loops are made by twisting a small piece of wire into a loop and pre-tinning before attaching to a seam on the back side. Two hanging loops are recommended for larger angels. The placement of loops is shown on pattern as dotted gray lines.

- Dotted lines indicate that pattern pieces are layered to give a three-dimensional effect. The special instructions included on the pattern page will explain how to layer the glass.

Layered glass section

Where layering occurs, complete the underlying pieces first. Clean to remove flux, then patina in that area if desired. Then attach the pieces that go on top and tack solder to a seam edge under them. Finish by cleaning entire piece, adding patina and then polishing.

- Copper foil overlays are used on some angels to form hair curls, sleeve bows, neck bow on the lamb, etc. The copper foil overlays are attached to solder seams and lightly tinned.

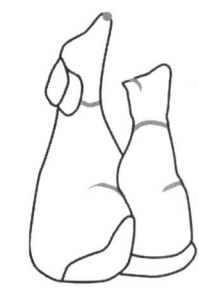
Copper foil overlays for collars, ear and haunches

- You might choose to give your angel personality by adding a face. We recommend painting with hobby enamel after your angel is finished and cleaned.

Painted face

- Some patterns have been reduced in size from the original. Suggesteded size will be given with each pattern . . . or build your angel to the size you like best!

Tip: Speed up construction by cutting many skirt pieces from one glass piece, then dividing it into sections according to the pattern. Many wing pieces were also cut this way - it makes for less grinding and a tighter seam fit, and also uses less glass. It is helpful to work over a light box using this method so that cut lines can be easily seen through the glass.

Precious

- Cut "curl" from foil. Attach where indicated by gray on pattern. Tin with solder.

Suggested size: Size shown

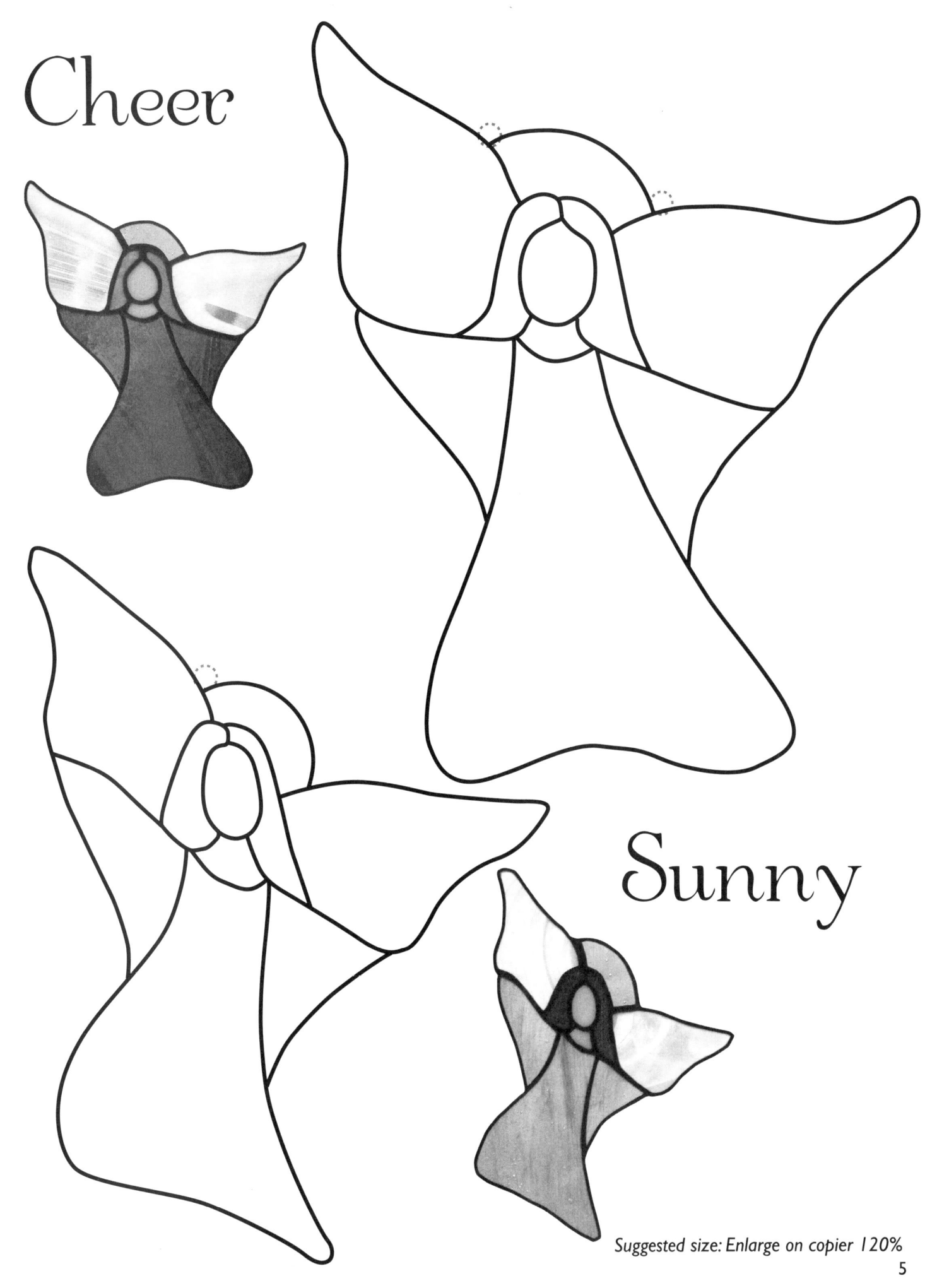

Cheer

Sunny

Suggested size: Enlarge on copier 120%

Tranquility

- Use a blue and green streaky art glass to best portray the "Earth" that the angel is cradling.

Suggested size: Enlarge on copier 120%

Guardian

- Personalize with a name painted onto the finished piece with hobby paint.

Suggested size: Enlarge on copier 120%

Compassion

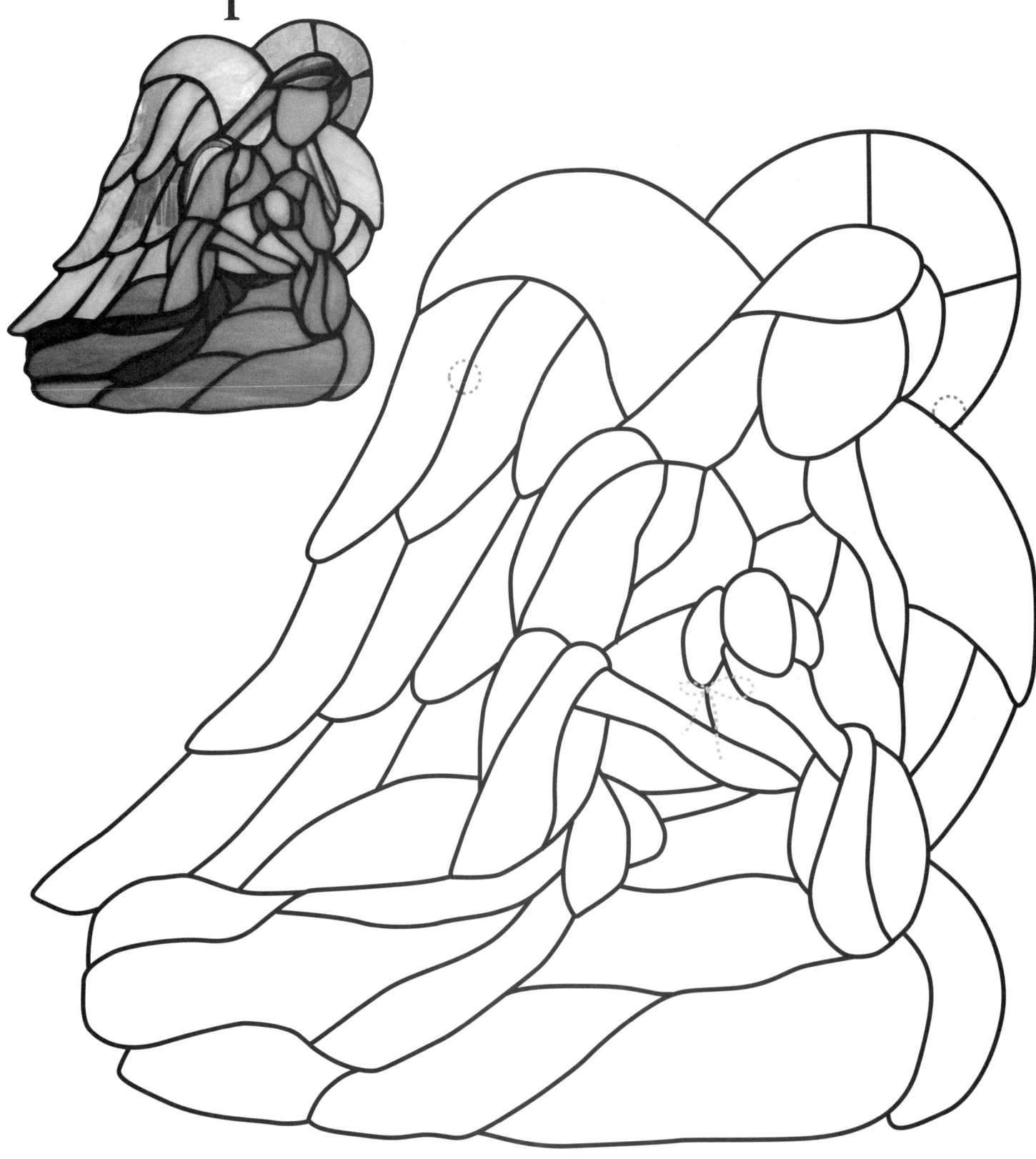

Optional: A tinned wire bow can be soldered to the lamb's neck to disguise the seam if desired.

Suggested size: Enlarge on copier 120%

Serenity

Optional: A heart, flower, crystal or other ornament can be glued on top of hands where indicated by star if desired.

Suggested size: Enlarge on copier 110%

Devotion

Suggested size: Size shown

Faith

Suggested size: Enlarge on copier 155%

Joy

For an added 3-D effect, a crystal can be soldered or glued onto hands.

Suggested size: Enlarge on copier 140%

Hope

Construct the bird separately by adding copper foil shapes to backs of pieces as indicated, then overlaying wing onto body and tack soldering. Tack solder bird to the hand after angel is completed, cleaned and patinaed.

Suggested size: Enlarge on copier 155%

Gaiety

The hair curl, bodice decoration and "bows" are copper foil overlays.

Suggested size: Enlarge on copier 155%

Loyalty

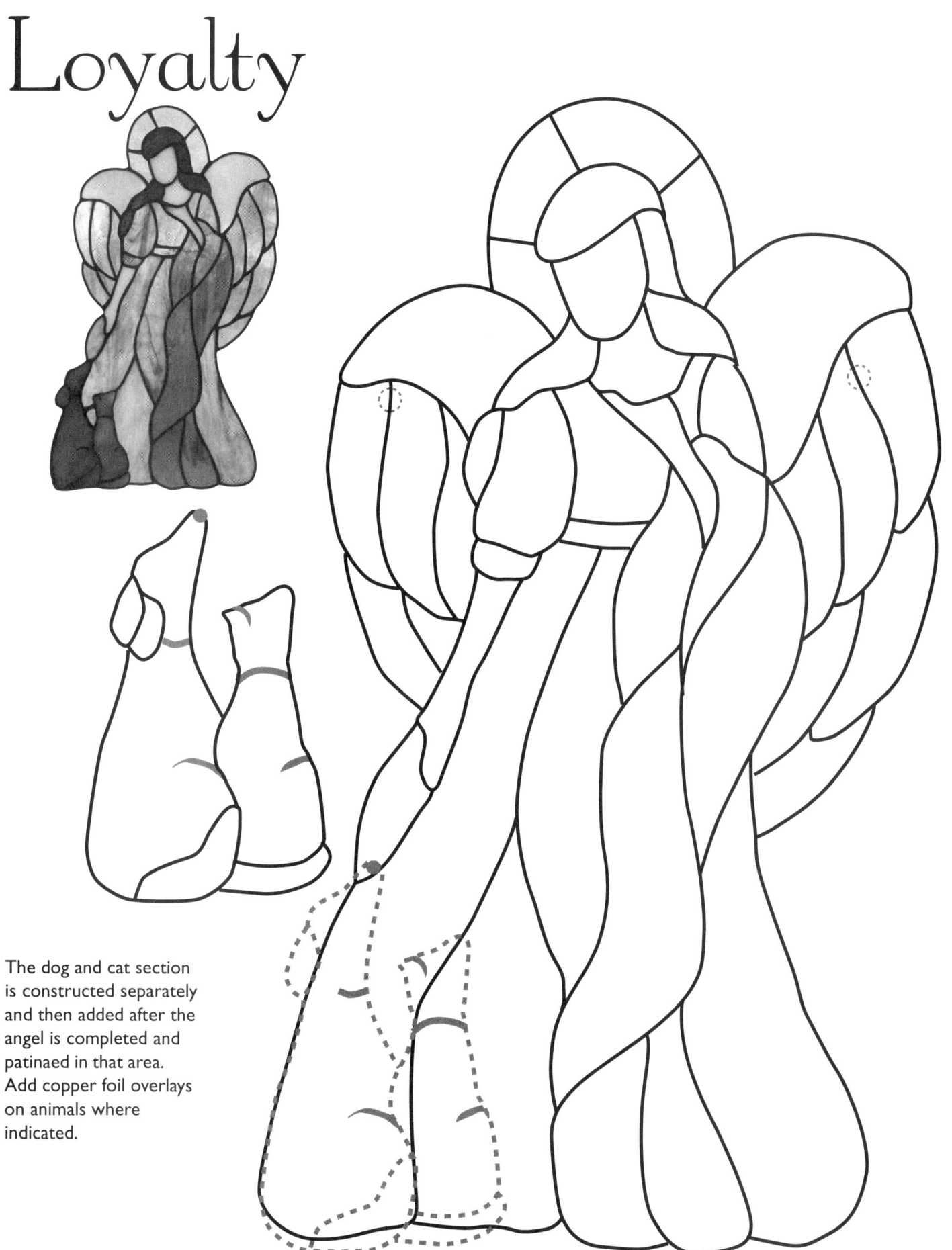

The dog and cat section is constructed separately and then added after the angel is completed and patinaed in that area. Add copper foil overlays on animals where indicated.

Suggested size: Enlarge on copier 155%

Madonna

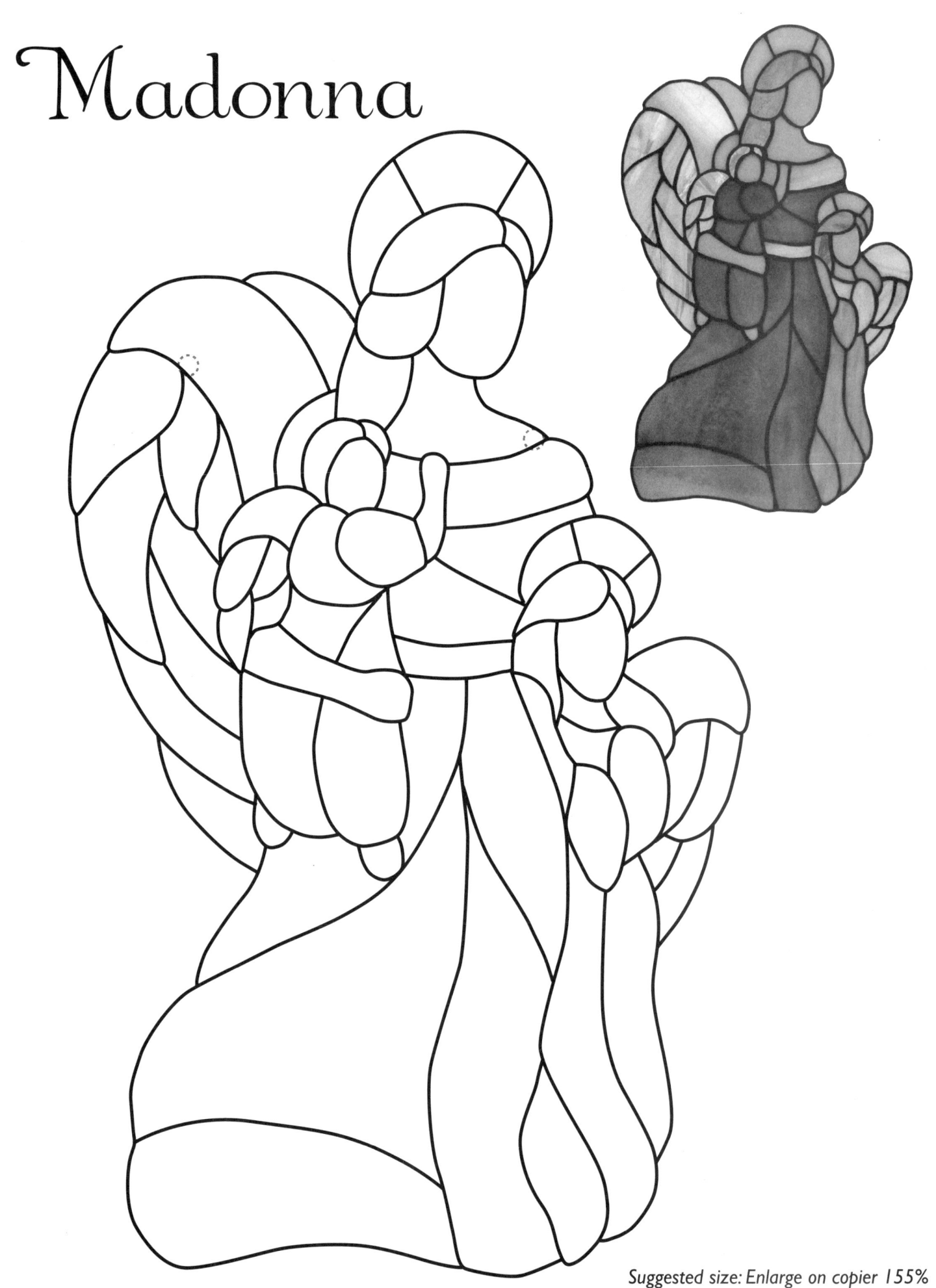

Suggested size: Enlarge on copier 155%

Blessing
Pages 26 & 27

Serenity
Page 9

Gratitude
Page 21

Compassion
Page 8

Suggested size: Enlarge on copier 165%

Praise

Build angel and arms separately. Arms are then overlaid on top of the wing pieces using the overlapping technique explained in the basic instructions. Tack solder from the back in several places.

Suggested size: Enlarge on copier 130%

Grace

Build angel and wings separately. Overlay angel on top of the wing pieces using the overlapping technique explained in the basic instructions. Tack solder from the back in several places.

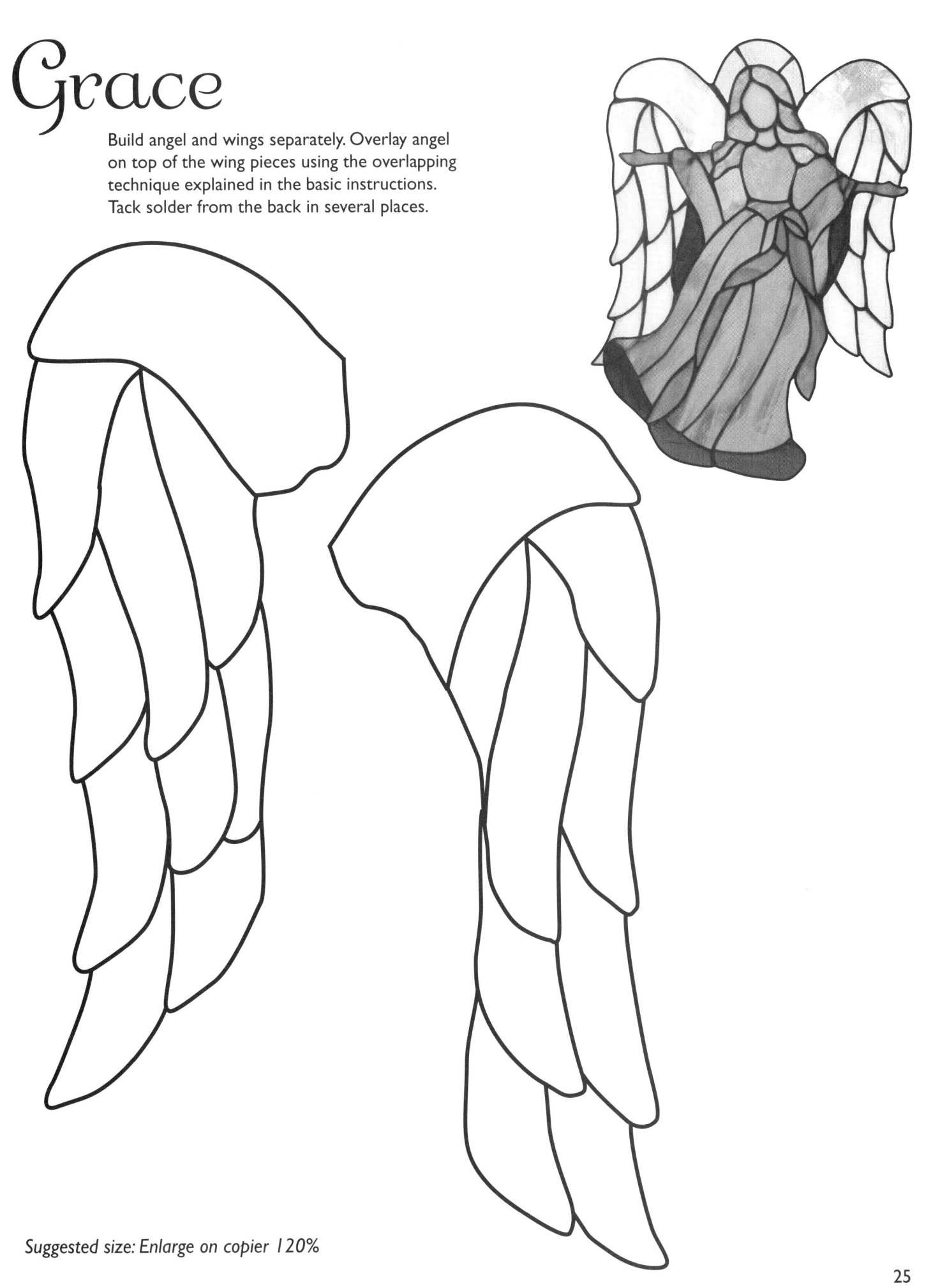

Suggested size: Enlarge on copier 120%

Suggested size: Enlarge on copier 155%

Blessing

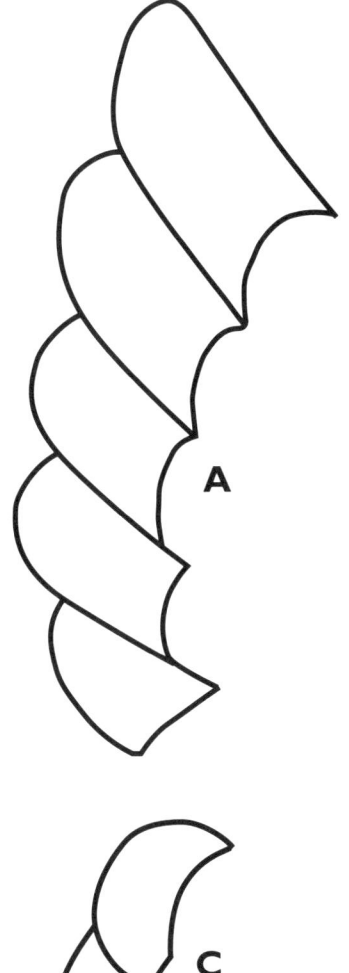
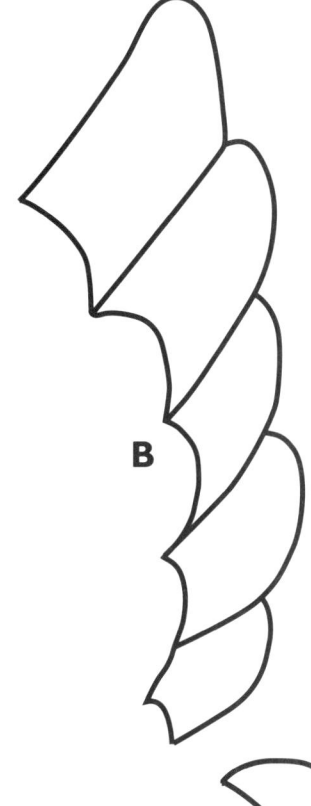

- Build angel. Clean, patina and polish.
- Build dove by adding copper foil shapes to backs of pieces as indicated, then overlaying wing onto body and tack soldering from behind. Tack solder olive branch to back of bird at beak. Clean and patina.
- Build wing sections (above). Clean and patina.
- Tack solder wing sections A & B in place to back of angel. Tack solder wing sections C & D onto front of angel.
- Tack solder dove onto front of angel.
- Do a final clean, spot patina and polish.

Spring

Build angel. Add wire overlays to the bunny ear and tail as indicated by the dotted line. Add a solder drop for the nose. The angel's necklace is made from a thin wire that is looped in the center, filled with solder and attached at neck seams.

Build wing section (below). Clean and patina angel and wing section, then overlay wing section over angel and tack solder securely from back. Clean, spot patina and polish.

Suggested size: Enlarge on copier 155%

Summer

The hair flower is a curled wire tinned and tack soldered to the hair seam. The stamens are made with twisted heavy gauge wire. Add solder drops to the end, then solder all stamens into the skirt seam.

Suggested size: Enlarge on copier 155%

29

Autumn

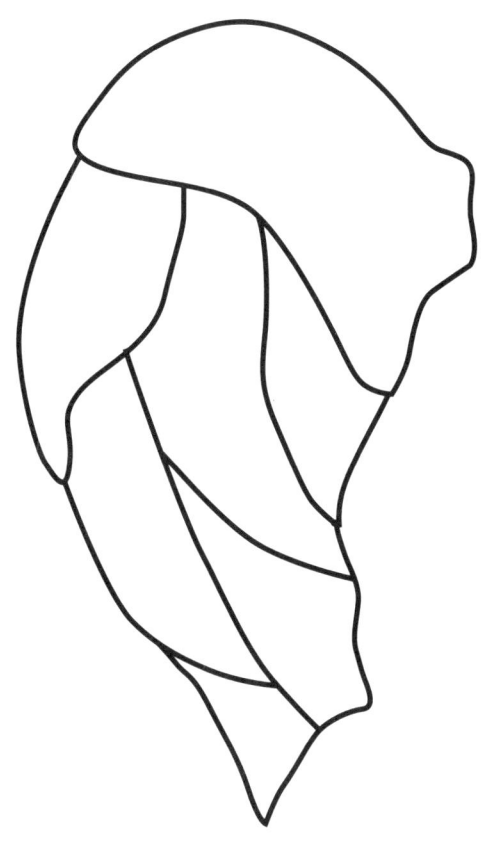

- The leaves on the skirt are cut with a band saw. Or grind inside curves with a small grinder bit. Add all veins with copper foil overlays cut with a hobby knife. Or use wire overlays for the veins.

- Build wings separately and solder to back of angel as explained in Basic Instructions on page 3.

- "Fruit" in basket are glass nuggets foiled and loosely tack soldered into open space. Finish by adding a circle piece behind them to form the bottom of the basket.

Suggested size: Enlarge on copier 150%

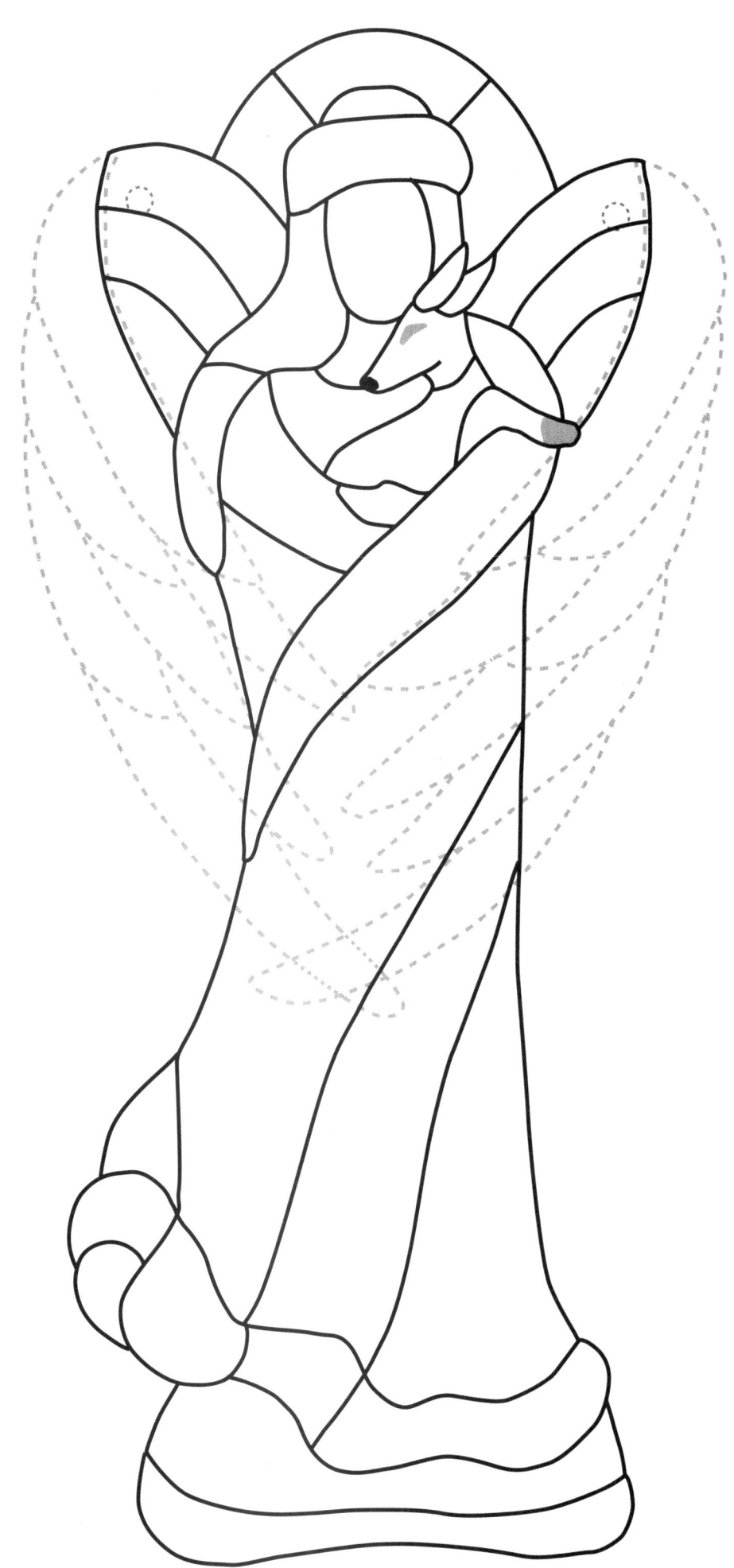

Winter

- Build angel and wing sections separately. After angel is finished, completely clean and patina the places where the wings will attach. Place a plain piece of scrap glass under wings to elevate so wing pieces can be soldered flat onto the skirt section. Tack solder together at the base where the wings touch the skirt.

- Add a solder drop for the deer's nose. The deer's eye, chin piece and hoof can be painted on with hobby paint. (Follow manufacturer's instructions.) Or use copper foil overlay for the features.

Suggested size: Enlarge on copier 135%

Champion

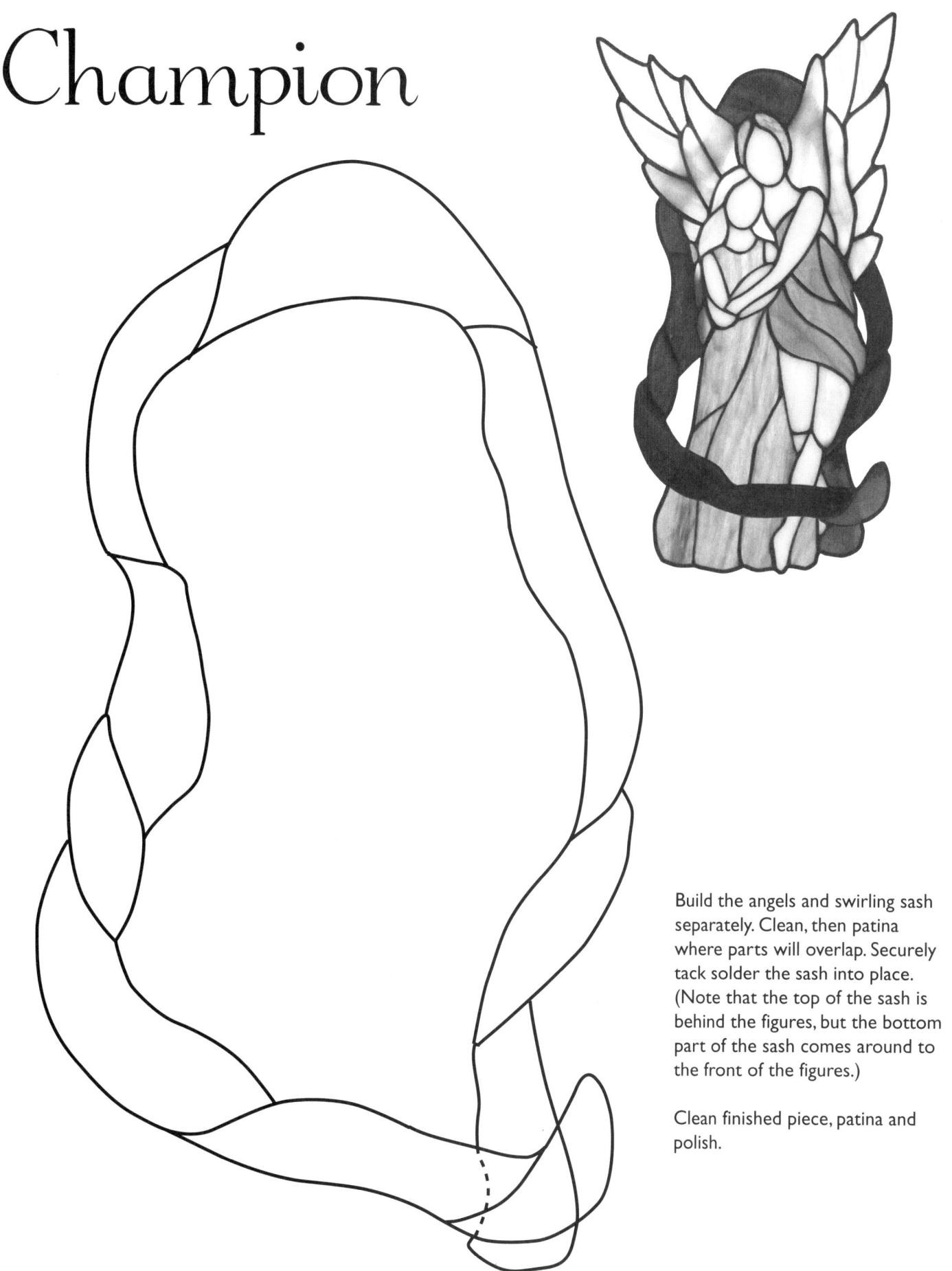

Build the angels and swirling sash separately. Clean, then patina where parts will overlap. Securely tack solder the sash into place. (Note that the top of the sash is behind the figures, but the bottom part of the sash comes around to the front of the figures.)

Clean finished piece, patina and polish.

Suggested size: Enlarge on copier 130%

Security

Build the angel and wing section separately. Clean, then patina where parts will overlap. Securely tack solder the wing section over the angel as shown. Clean finished piece, patina and polish. "Curl" shown in gray is a foil overlay.

Suggested size: Enlarge on copier 130%